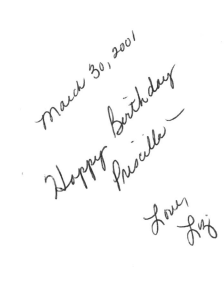

March 30, 2001

Happy Birthday
Priscilla—

Love,
Liz

To:

_____

From:

_____

Patterns *of* Grace

The Wonderful Ways God's Love
Touches Our Lives

FRONTPORCH
BOOKS™

Copyright ©1999 by Roy Lessin and Heather Solum
Published by FrontPorch Books, a division of Garborg's, LLC
P.O. Box 20132, Bloomington, MN 55420

Design by Garborg Design Works

Unless otherwise noted, all scripture verses are taken
from the Holy Bible, King James Version.

Scripture quotations marked NIV are taken from the
Holy Bible, New International Version®.
Copyright © 1973, 1978, 1984 by International Bible Society.
Used by permission of Zondervan Publishing House.

Nine Patch Quilt hand-made by *Chris Smith*, St. Paul, Minnesota.

ISBN 1-58375-464-4

Printed in Mexico.

Table of Contents

Introduction

God is the Master Craftsman. His work is priceless and His results are matchless. We see the majesty and awesome splendor of His work each time we stand upon a mountain, look upon a meadow, stand before an ocean, or gaze into the heavens. Above all this, nothing compares to the beauty of the work that His transforming grace does within the human heart. Grace is a work of love. It is a work of goodness, kindness, and endless generosity. Through it we find peace and purpose and a thousand reasons to rejoice. Through the work that God is doing in us we can see the patterns of His grace. Like a quilter, God is using every stitch and every piece of our lives to create in us the image of His Son.

Patchwork Quilt *The Blessings*

The Patchwork Quilt is uniquely American. It first

appeared in the early 1800s, breaking away from

the formal patterns of the past. Its creation was

promoted by the scarcity of materials and the harsh

realities of daily frontier life. Pieced together from

whatever materials were available, the main purpose

for a patchwork quilt was not to decorate a home,

but to keep the family warm. It also provided a

practical way for a frontier wife and mother to

express her love for her family through the work

of her hands.

# of Home

Home Is Where…hearts are united, hands are joined, character is formed, truth is spoken, values are established, care is given, love serves all.

For he hath strengthened the bars of thy gates;
he hath blessed thy children within thee.
PSALM 147:13

Bundle me up in
an old, worn quilt
with hand-sewn
stitches and soft
cotton batting—
place a book on my
lap, a cup of tea in
my hand, a light by
my side, and leave
me in a world of rest
and delight.

You can never have too many quilts.

GRACE IS

SOMETHING

OUR HEARTS

Come with me by yourselves to a quiet place and get some rest.
MARK 6:31 NIV

CAN SNUGGLE

UP TO.

Oh! There's a power to make each hour as sweet as Heaven designed it;

Nor need we roam to bring it home, though few there be that find it:

Love turns a house into a home…grace turns a home into a haven.

We seek too high for things close by, and lose what nature found us,

For life hath here no gifts so dear as home and friends around us.

SWAN

And God is able to make all grace abound toward you; that ye, always having all sufficiency in all things, may abound to every good work.

2 CORINTHIANS 9:8

The quilt of God's love that covers us is custom-made by His skilled hands. The pattern is one of a kind. It is formed by joining the various pieces of our lives and fitting them together into a beautiful expression of His craftsmanship. The softness of its batting comes from the

gentleness of His ways. The quilt's warmth

assures us of His constant care. The finished

work is priceless and will become a cherished

part of our family's heritage to be passed on

from generation to generation.

My life is handmade—
My heart is homespun!

The home improves

happiness and

abates misery by

doubling our joy

and dividing

our grief!

ADDISON

18

G RACE
fills our lives with good things,

G RACE
is a gift from above—

G RACE
fills our home with beauty,

G RACE
fills our hearts with love.

From the fullness

of his grace we have

all received one blessing

after another.

JOHN 1:16 NIV

Schoolhouse Quilt

Applying Our

This nostalgic pattern dates back to the 1850s and was loved by many, becoming a favorite among quilters of all ages. Because of its simple lines, smaller versions were often made by children learning the art of quilting. Today, more than a dozen variations of this box quilt pattern exist.

Hearts to Wisdom

May the favor of the Lord

our God rest upon us;

establish the work of

our hands for us—

yes, establish the work

of our hands.

PSALM 90:17 NIV

24

Hands To Serve

My hands can serve as He served—

to raise someone who has fallen...

to support someone who is weak...

to uphold someone who is weary.

To wipe a tear...to hold a hand...to give a cup of water.

To embrace...to carry a burden...to impart a blessing.

Lord, use my hands.

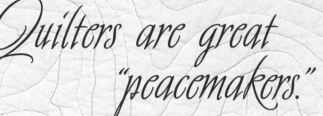

Quilters are great "peacemakers."

Quilters
make
wonderful
comforters.

Let the word of Christ dwell

in you richly in all wisdom;

teaching and admonishing

one another in psalms and

hymns and spiritual songs,

singing with grace in your

hearts to the Lord.

COLOSSIANS 3:16

Wise mothers and grandmothers used quilting

as a way to teach young girls the important

values of industry, economy, and thrift.

Teach us to number our days, that we
may apply our hearts unto wisdom.

PSALM 90:12

To create a handmade quilt is not a
rush job. Quilting takes time, care,
and patience. In God's graciousness
He is caring, patient, and kind with
us. He sees the end result of His work
in us and knows it is worth the wait.

In all things

showing thyself

a pattern of

good works.

TITUS 2:7

To every thing there is

a season, and a time to

every purpose under the

heaven…a time to sew.

Every quilt that
has been made by
skilled and caring
hands has a story
to tell; so does
every life that
is a work of
the Master's
gracious hands.

See that you

make them

according to

the pattern

shown you.

EXODUS 25:40 NIV

Behind every handmade quilt is a quilter. Quilters made

quilts for specific purposes, including dowries, fund-raising,

celebrations, and education. No quilt exists by accident.

You are God's creation, and He has a specific purpose for

your life. It is the perfect purpose, designed for you alone

and never to be repeated.

Gracefulness is expressed by a heart full of graciousness.

Someone who is wise sees

life through God's revelation,

makes choices based upon

God's instruction, and walks

according to God's direction.

37

Wedding Ring Quilt
The Beautiful

A bride's hope chest usually held as many as 12 different quilts lovingly made by family and friends. The Wedding Ring Quilt was a prized gift given to a bride and groom in celebration of their wedding day. The joining and intertwining of the circles within the Wedding Ring pattern symbolizes the biblical declaration that two lives become one flesh through the union of marriage.

Ways of Love

Quilts are like letters that share someone's thoughts...

like books that tell someone's story...

like journals that reflect someone's heart.

Lives touched
by God's grace
sew love.

Old family quilts never lose

the scent of a Grandma's love.

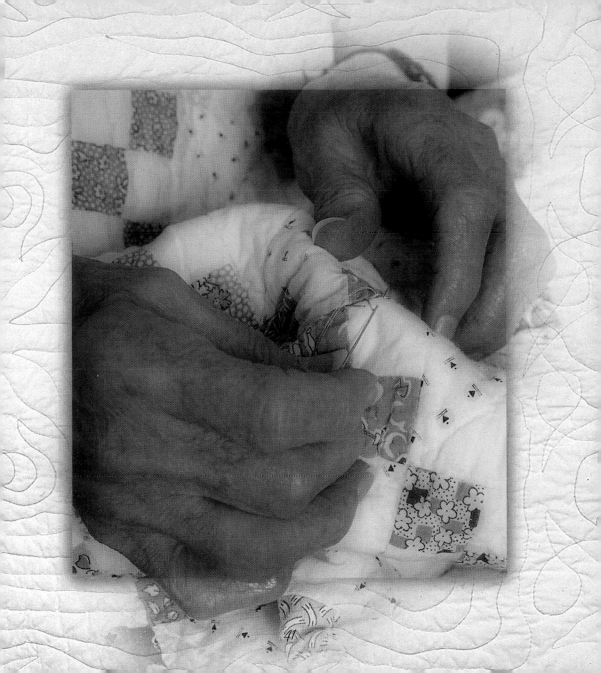

IN THE QUILT
OF LIFE, GOD
HAS JOINED
MY HEART
TO YOURS.

God made a woman by forming

her with His hands—

when she became a mother, she

was touched by God's heart.

Family quilts are never
strangers, but friends with
whom we are familiar
and that lovingly tie us
to our past.

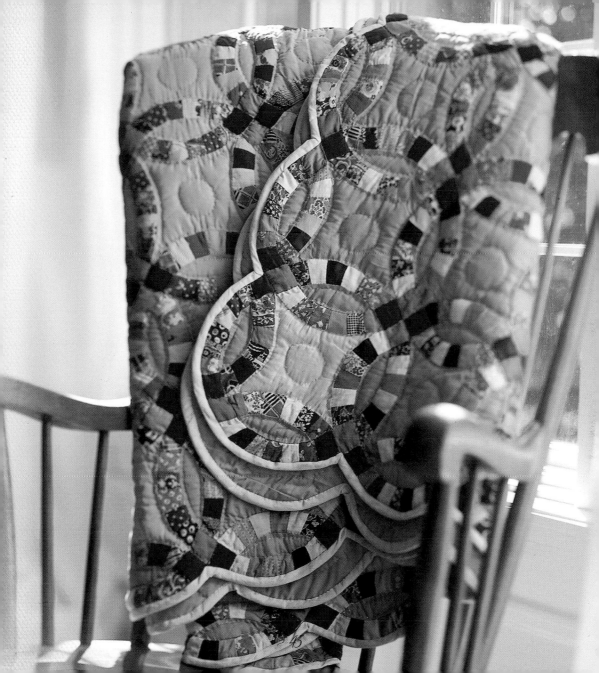

The things quilts sew into our hearts—

threads of common joys and treasured memories,

pieces of cherished conversations and shared secrets,

colors of rich smiles and endless laughter,

patterns of friendship and love's sweet rewards.

Hidden within the

stitches of a quilt

are the hopes and dreams

that a mother holds

Home is where there's one to love;

for her children.

Home is where there's one to love us!

47

Deeds of kindness, done in love,

Diamonds are in settings rare;

In the realms of bliss above

These the gems the blessed wear.

Let us cherish them with care

Looks and words and deeds of love,

Each the other's burden bear,

Traveling to our home above.

Song Garden

A house becomes a home

when each room is clothed with peace,

each wall is covered with laughter,

and each heart is filled with love.

It is a good thing that the heart be established with grace.

HEBREWS 13:9

Crazy Quilt
All Things Work

Even though its name implies something haphazard,
this quilt is far from being undesirable. Mixture is
at the heart of the Crazy Quilt, combining various
patterns, colors, and fabrics. The Crazy Quilt
maker brings all of these varying elements together
for a common good and a useful purpose. The Crazy
Quilt experienced huge popularity
during the Victorian era, when wealthy women
adorned them with expensive fabrics and elaborate
decorations. Today it remains a popular decorating
theme in country homes.

Together for Good

As we look at the pattern of God's grace

upon our lives we discover an endless seam

of benefits, delights, and comforts.

The grace of God has been
given to us in such abundance
that no one could ever express
more goodness to us...
shower more kindness upon us...
or carry more tenderness toward us.

Grace WILL NOT FAIL TO COMFORT YOU…

WILL NOT CEASE TO CARE FOR YOU…

WILL NOT KEEP FROM COVERING YOU,

WITH ALL THAT IS IN THE HEART OF *God.*

A tattered quilt does not mean that it has lost its usefulness, for its maker knows how to skillfully mend it and make it useful again.

*Like a quilt,
grace wraps us in
comfort, allowing
us to daily rest
in the goodness
of the Lord.*

God's heart forms the
pattern that He is using in
our lives, and the eyes of
faith see His gracious work.

GOD IS MAKING YOU

INTO A GRACIOUS EXPRESSION

OF HIS LOVE, DESIGN,

AND ORIGINALITY.

My grace is sufficient for thee: for my

strength is made perfect in weakness.

2 CORINTHIANS 12:9

Grace takes the "crazy quilt" pattern of our lives and turns it into God's beautiful design.

For the Lord God is a sun and shield:

the Lord will give grace and glory:

THE RESULT OF GOD'S GRACE IN

no good thing will he withhold

YOUR LIFE IS A "WORK OF HEART."

from them that walk uprightly.

PSALM 84:11

We are his workmanship. EPHESIANS 2:10

Nothing is wasted in our lives when God does His "peace work."

A quilter's skilled hands know how to create something

beautiful and practical out of scraps, making something of

value from something that would normally be discarded.

How much more does God, the Master Craftsman,

make something beautiful out of our tattered lives

when we give Him all the pieces.

Friendship Quilt The Gift of

Long ago, the Friendship Quilt served as a reminder of the friendships and special relationships that existed within a community. These quilts were lovingly prepared for times of celebration or as a means of expressing care and appreciation. Newly married couples heading for the frontier, pastors, and even school teachers were among those who benefited from this meaningful tradition. Today, anyone who has inherited or purchased one of these treasured quilts possesses a special part of our country's history.

Friendship

Friendship is a collection

of kindly thoughts,

of love-rich seeds,

of heartfelt words,

and caring deeds.

If I could search for one true friend

and seek until the very end,

I'd find out what I always knew—

there is no better friend than you.

God…gives grace to the humble.

JAMES 4:6 NIV

There is no greater friendship than the one that exists between a person and God.

God looks for the earth and every good thing in it belongs to the Lord. God is yours to enjoy.

Pb

Man does the planting and watering…but God is the one who makes things grow!

OUTREACH OAKS

YOU ARE GOD'S GARDEN. I COR. 3:7

Gail

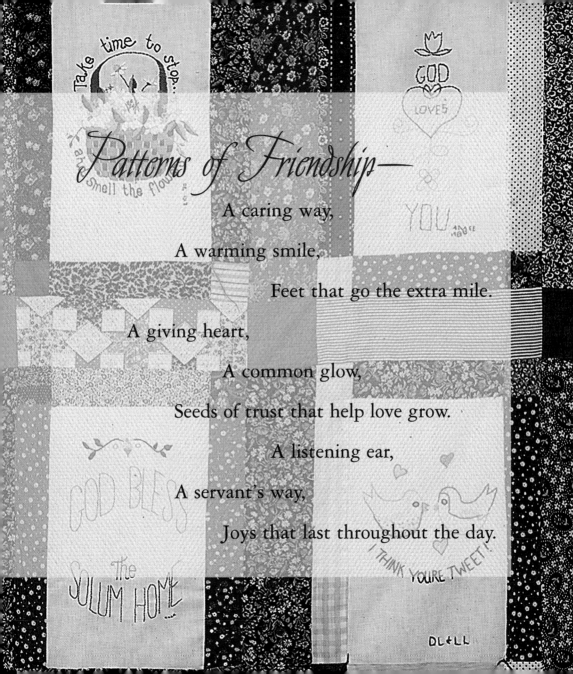

Patterns of Friendship—

A caring way,

A warming smile,

Feet that go the extra mile.

A giving heart,

A common glow,

Seeds of trust that help love grow.

A listening ear,

A servant's way,

Joys that last throughout the day.

Friendship is like

a warm, cozy quilt—

stitched with a thousand

threads of joy.

A FRIEND INCREASES YOUR

JOYS AND LIGHTENS YOUR LOAD.

In the golden chain

of friendship regard

me as a link.

SEWN ON AN

ANTIQUE FRIENDSHIP QUILT

BY IDA HOOPER, QUILTER

The best friends are old friends.

*Let your
conversation
be always
full of grace.*

<small>COLOSSIANS 4:6 NIV</small>

When grace is in our

hearts our words will be

softer, kinder, purer, sweeter.

Omniscience means

that God knows

everything about you.

Grace means that God

knows everything

about you, and loves

you still.

PRAISE FOR THE EARTH AND EVERY GOOD THING IN IT. BLESS IS THE LORD. GOD IS YOURS TO ENJOY.

Pb

Man does the planting and watering...but God is the one who makes things grow!

you are God's garden. I COR 3:7

OUTREACH OAKS

Take time to stop...
and smell the flowers!

A true friend
warms you with
her presence,
trusts you with
her secrets and
remembers you
in her prayers.

GOD
LOVES
&
YOU

In my Father's
house there are many
mansions. I hope
mine is next to yours.

GOD BLESS
The
SOLUM HOME

I THINK YOU'RE TWEET!

Grace

IS THE SOIL FROM WHICH

HEALTHY FRIENDSHIPS GROW.

Grace be with you, mercy, and peace,

from God the Father, and from

the Lord Jesus Christ, the Son of the

Father, in truth and love.

2 JOHN 1:3

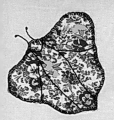

Butterfly Quilt New Lives,

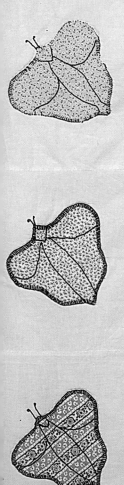

The delight that we find in the butterfly is due not only to the beauty of its wings and graceful flight, but also to its transformation from a creature of the earth to a creature of the sky. The popular butterfly theme appeared on quilts through a technique know as appliqué—cutting pieces of one material and applying them to the surface of another. This differs from patchwork quilts which use geometric designs that are stitched together. The look of an appliqué quilt differs from a patchwork quilt, but the end result is still warmth and comfort.

New Beginnings

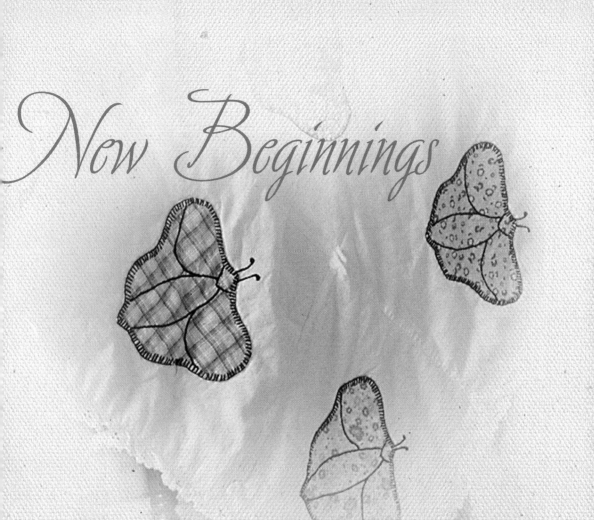

In loving ways, piece by piece, God's hand applies His work of

grace to our lives—transforming us into something beautiful.

THE WORK OF GOD'S
GRACE IN OUR LIVES
IS A HEART-SOFTENER.

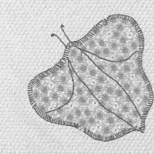

Grace and peace be yours in abundance.

2 PETER 1:2 NIV

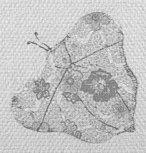

God extended His
grace to you when you
did not know Him,
and He will not cease
to be gracious to you
now that you are His.

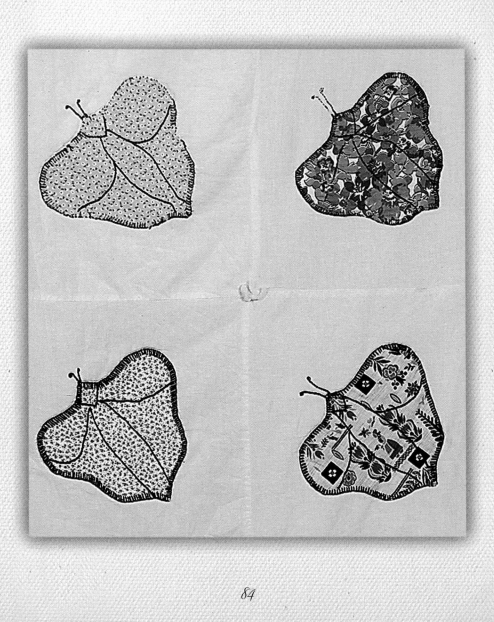

GOD POURED ALL OF HIS GRACE INTO JESUS, AND JESUS HAS POURED ALL OF HIS GRACE UPON YOU.

Amazing grace! how sweet the sound—that saved a wretch like me!

I once was lost but now am found, was blind but now I see.

'Twas grace that taught my heart to fear, and grace my fears relieved;

How precious did that grace appear the hour I first believed.

Through many dangers, toils, and snares, I have already come;

'Tis grace has brought me safe thus far, and grace will lead me home.

The Lord has promised good to me, His word my hope secures;

He will my shield and portion be as long as life endures.

JOHN NEWTON

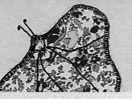

The best way to begin a
day is by opening our hearts
to God's resources—
His supply is endless,
His grace is measureless,
His love is matchless.

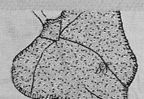

GOD HAS SOMETHING

NEW FOR YOU

EVERY DAY.

HE DELIGHTS

IN YOU AND

LOVES TO

SURPRISE YOU

WITH

GOOD THINGS.

*B*ecause God is, there is grace…and because there is grace, there is hope…and because there is hope, we can put energy into our day, faith into our prayers, joy into our worship, confidence into our calling, and zeal into our step.

As we walk with God
each day He will do
His work within us,
peace by peace, by peace.

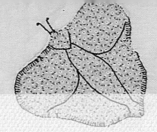

Grace

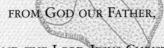

TO YOU AND PEACE

FROM GOD OUR FATHER,

AND THE LORD JESUS CHRIST.

ROMANS 1:7

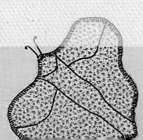

Americana Quilt
God Bless

Since the colors red, white, and blue were chosen for the American flag they have come to represent the freedom on which our country was founded. Along with other symbols of freedom, such as the eagle and the liberty bell, these colors have been incorporated into quilts with pride. They speak of celebration and victory, of our history and heritage, and of our birth as a nation. For all of the immigrants that came to this great country to gain freedom, these patriotic quilts became an important way to express the love they had for their country.

America

America is great because God has been gracious to her.

Blessed is the nation whose

God is the Lord: and the

people whom he hath chosen

for his own inheritance.

PSALM 33:12

RIGHTEOUSNESS
EXALTS A NATION.

PROVERBS 14:34 NIV

One day a grandmother wanted to find something to occupy her active twelve-year-old granddaughter. She found a picture of a quilt with the pattern of America on it that included all the states. She showed the picture to her granddaughter, and then proceeded to cut it into many pieces. "Now," replied the grandmother, "See if you can put our country back together again." Instead of taking a long time to complete, the granddaughter returned the picture taped together and in complete order in a few short minutes. "How did you do that so quickly?" asked the grandmother. "It was easy," answered the granddaughter, "Before you cut it up I noticed that there was a picture of a little girl on the back. When I put the girl together I knew I had put the country back together."

I know three things must always be to keep a nation strong and free.

One is a hearthstone bright and dear, with busy, happy loved ones near.

One is a ready heart and hand to love, and serve, and keep the land.

One is a worn and beaten way to where the people go to pray.

So long as these are kept alive, nation and people will survive.

God keep them always, everywhere: the hearth, the flag, the place of prayer.

UNKNOWN

One nation under God.

There is nothing
greater that can
be upon a nation,
a people, a family,
or a person than the
blessing and goodness
of God.

THE FABRIC OF
A GREAT NATION
IS FOUND IN THE

truth

OF ITS FOUNDATIONS, THE

character

OF ITS LEADERS, THE

faith

OF ITS PEOPLE, AND THE

love

OF ALL.

Let us have faith

that right makes

might; and in that

faith let us dare to

do our duty as we

understand it.

Abraham Lincoln

I sought for the greatness of America

in her harbors and rivers and fertile fields.

It was not there. Not until I went

into the churches and heard her pulpits

flame with righteousness did I

understand the greatness of her power.

DE TOCQUEVILLE OF FRANCE

WHATEVER MAKES MEN GOOD CHRISTIANS,
MAKES THEM GOOD CITIZENS.

DANIEL WEBSTER

The Bible is a book of faith,

and a book of doctrine,

and a book of morals,

and a book of religion,

of especial revelation from God.

DANIEL WEBSTER

I believe the Bible is the best gift God has ever given to man. All the good from the Savior of the world is communicated through this book.... All things desirable to men are contained in the Bible.

ABRAHAM LINCOLN

It is impossible to rightly govern the world without God and the Bible.

GEORGE WASHINGTON

108

LORD, MAKE OUR COUNTRY

LIKE A QUILT IN YOUR HANDS—

SHAPED BY YOUR WILL,

USED FOR YOUR PURPOSE,

JOINED BY YOUR GRACE,

HELD TOGETHER BY YOUR LOVE.

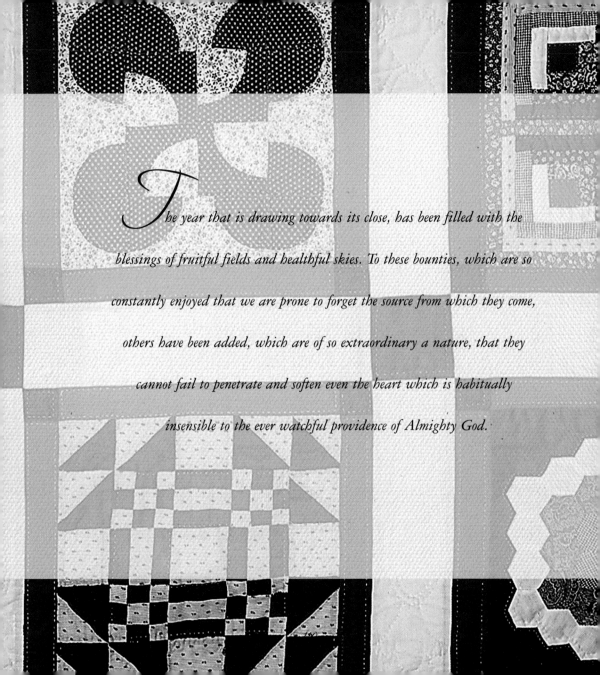

The year that is drawing towards its close, has been filled with the blessings of fruitful fields and healthful skies. To these bounties, which are so constantly enjoyed that we are prone to forget the source from which they come, others have been added, which are of so extraordinary a nature, that they cannot fail to penetrate and soften even the heart which is habitually insensible to the ever watchful providence of Almighty God.

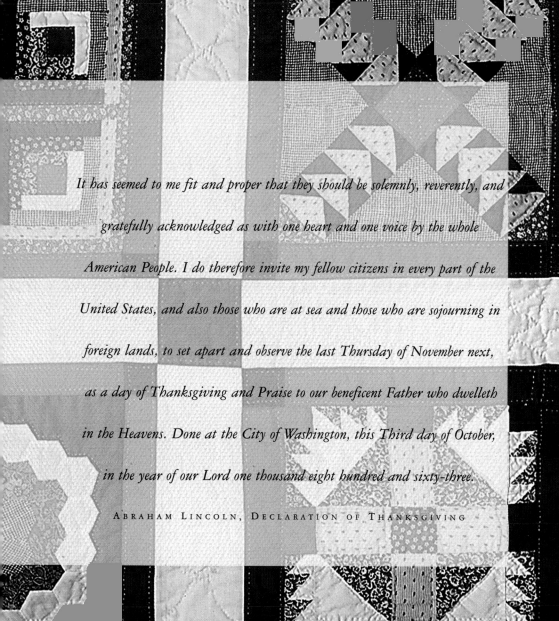

It has seemed to me fit and proper that they should be solemnly, reverently, and

gratefully acknowledged as with one heart and one voice by the whole

American People. I do therefore invite my fellow citizens in every part of the

United States, and also those who are at sea and those who are sojourning in

foreign lands, to set apart and observe the last Thursday of November next,

as a day of Thanksgiving and Praise to our beneficent Father who dwelleth

in the Heavens. Done at the City of Washington, this Third day of October,

in the year of our Lord one thousand eight hundred and sixty-three.

ABRAHAM LINCOLN, DECLARATION OF THANKSGIVING

America,
America,
God shed
His grace
on thee.

Nine Patch Quilt

Seasons of Life

This quilt received its name for its use of patches made of nine squares of fabric. Two different fabrics were used for each patch. The quilt was assembled to produce a beautiful patterned work of art using fabric scraps. Its finished look was a true work of art and took many hours of planning and preparation. Projects like these helped keep quilters innovative, creative, and imaginative, and the hours they invested brought so much beauty to others.

Birth

Quilts do not appear by chance—
they are made by a designer,
and the designer has a specific
purpose in mind for the quilt
that is being created.

Only a creative God could make creative people.

I will praise thee; for I am fearfully and
wonderfully made: marvellous are thy works;
and that my soul knoweth right well.

PSALM 139:14

Childhood

One of the wonders about

quilts is the beauty that

comes from their simplicity.

Verily I say unto you, Whosoever shall not receive the kingdom of God
as a little child, he shall not enter therein.

MARK 10:15

Train up a child in the way he should go:
and when he is old, he will not depart from it.

PROVERBS 22:6

Training

Quilting is a craft that can be learned by a willing heart, and perfected through a trained eye and skilled hands.

Youth

A quilt has its greatest value to
the one who personally knows
the quilter who made it.

*Remember now thy Creator
in the days of thy youth.*

ECCLESIASTES 12:1

Incline thine ear unto wisdom, and apply thine heart to understanding.

PROVERBS 2:2

Education A wise and skilled quilter has learned how to create a quilt of beauty with very little waste.

Marriage

A pattern-quilt cannot be successfully formed unless two pieces of material are purposefully joined together.

Home Like a cozy quilt,
home is a place
where you feel
warmed and
covered by love.

*In the house of the righteous
is much treasure.*

PROVERBS 15:6

122

Motherhood

American women have long spoken with their needles, and their voices are still being heard today.

Who can find a virtuous woman? for her price is far above rubies.

PROVERBS 31:10

No one can fully measure the blessings that come to the life of the one who has a praying mother.

Homemaking

One of the great joys of a quilter is knowing the pleasure and the benefits that her labor will bring to the one who receives it.

Every wise woman buildeth her house.
PROVERBS 14:1

Quilts are not only beautiful, they are practical.

Old Age

Old quilts are true family treasures because of all the love they convey and all the cherished memories they hold.

From the beginning of our days to the end of our years, through all of the patterns of life, all is by grace.

I WAS YOUNG

AND NOW I AM OLD

YET HAVE I NEVER SEEN

THE RIGHTEOUS FORSAKEN,

OR THEIR CHILDREN BEGGING BREAD.

PSALM 37:25 NIV

127

By the grace of God I am what I am.

1 Corinthians 15:10

May the grace of God
warm your heart,
day after day,
year after year,
over and over again.